# The Possibility of Joy: A Book of Poetry

By Jennifer Gurney

ISBN: 978-93-6354-148-1

First Edition: 2026
Rs. 200/-

Cyberwit.net
HIG 45 Kaushambi Kunj, Kalindipuram
Allahabad - 211011 (U.P.) India
http://www.cyberwit.net
Tel: +(91) 9415091004
E-mail: info@cyberwit.net



Printed at Repro India Limited.

## Dedication

*The Possibility of Joy: A Book of Poetry* is dedicated to my brother, Joe Heitman. We are only 18 months apart in age and he was my very first best friend. He is my only sibling, and throughout my life he has been a source of inspiration, understanding and encouragement. I love him to the moon and back and wish we lived closer. The poem *When I Retire to Michigan* holds memories of Joe at its very core. And the title of this book embodies his joie de vivre. If anyone embodies the possibility of joy, it's my brother Joe.

# Contents

**Previously published in The Ravens Perch 9-3-25**

## Grief's Lament

loneliness
joins me on the cool patio this morning
a constant friend

in the water spraying from the hose
onto my deadheaded rose bush
resting for a second bloom

in the mourning dove's aria
sung from the rooftop
to the neighborhood, and me, below

is it mourning dove
or morning dove
and does it really matter

in my cat
timidly tiptoeing through the threshold
to behold what treasures await

in the beams of sunshine
slanting across the bricks
just now reaching my toes

in the coffee's steam
that shows me just how cold it is
this morning

in the memories
ever present yet just a thought away
that bring you back to me

friends are everywhere
and nowhere
grief is funny that way

**Previously published in The Ravens Perch 9-3-25**

## What Breaks My Heart

it breaks my heart that you died
that you're gone
that you're never coming back

it breaks my heart that
I didn't get to see you before you died
you didn't want me to see you this way

it breaks my heart
that I will never hear you laugh again
ever, not even once

it breaks my heart
that I'll never smell your scent again
not even on the dark nights when I need to the most

it breaks my heart
that I'll never hear you say you love me again
when my heart so longs for your words

it breaks my heart
that I'll never spoon you again
or float on the fumes of our love

it breaks my heart
that you'll never read to me again
end-to-end on the sofa

it breaks my heart
that we'll never ride in the canyons again
yelling "woo hoo!" as we head to the high country

it breaks my heart
we'll never listen to music again
with your signing off key to my laughter

it breaks my heart
that the me that was me when I was with you
is gone along with you

the one who was free
and brave and whole … and loved
the one who was young with you

it breaks my heart
that you died and are never, ever
coming back

**Previously published in The Ravens Perch 9-3-25**

# Uncried

I have cried
tears that
once shed
and wiped away
cannot be
uncried

they pour
from my heart
my mind
my soul
which are all
grappling
to believe
that
you
are
actually
dead

my mind seeks proof
where none exists
save the lone phone call
from my stepson
the next morning

my heart
seeks closure
of saying
all the was in it
which, luckily
I was brave enough
to do

my soul
seeks respite
from the
exhaustion
of the
grueling work
of trying
to let
you go

I long to
de-cry
the tears

and have you
back again

**Previously published in The Ravens Perch 9-3-25**

## You Never Made it to Michigan

every time
I'd visit Michigan
in the summer
I'd invite you

you'd remind me
that you've never been
yet

and you'd say
I can't this year
maybe next time
Baby

every time we talked
about my dream
of retiring to Michigan
you'd remind me
that you've never been

and I would say
yet

well
I'm headed to Michigan
tomorrow
and it just hit me

that
I can't invite you
this year

it's too late

and

I can't invite you
with me when I retire
to Michigan
in four years
to start my dream of
a house on a lake
with an art center

it breaks my heart
that we
missed the chance

and

that you're
never going to
make it
to Michigan

I'll just have
to take you there
in my heart

**Previously published in The Ravens Perch 10-18-25**

# I Know

I know
it probably sounds silly
but eating with a spoon
that was once ours
with that heavy feel
that you really loved
makes me feel, through the tears
closer to you

I know
it probably sounds silly
but listening to your voice mails
on my old phone
where you say "Hey, Baby"
and "I love you"
in every one
makes me feel, through the tears
closer to you

I know
it probably sounds silly
but I can't bring myself
to throw away your ratty sneakers
that live in the garage, still
them hanging around
makes me feel, through the tears
closer to you

I know
it probably sounds silly
but I still buy your favorite soap
and laundry detergent
and shampoo
because your scent lingers longer
and makes me feel, through the tears
closer to you

I know
it probably sounds silly
but I still only buy
your two favorite flavors of ice cream
Ben and Jerry's Cherry Garcia
and Breyer's Chocolate
just one bite
makes me feel, through the tears
closer to you

**Previously published in The Ravens Perch 10-18-25**

# I Long

I long
to shed the layers
of grief

one at a time
baring new skin
each time, to heal

until at last
my skin is newly thick enough
to carry joy alongside grief

**Previously published in The Ravens Perch 10-18-25**

# Is There Room

is there room
on the back of your bike
for one last ride

is there time for
one last woo hoo
as we peel out of the driveway

my arms
circled around you
leaning into every curve

your left hand
on my leg
claiming me

is there time
for one last ride up the canyon
to see the leaves, golden

winding
our arms outstretched like birds
floating down the canyon

falling
deeper in love
with every ride

is there room
on the back of the bike
for one last ride

tears streaming down my cheeks
high on life and at the top of the world
all leather and lace

I will feel
my arms tight around you
holding on forever

**Previously published in The Ravens Perch 10-24-25**

## Sometimes You Have to Touch the Bruise to Heal

I walked around the lake today
for the first time
since you died

the lake where
we
lived

the lake where
we
built our deck

the lake where
we
got married

the lake where
we
built a life together

the lake where
your
memorial bench will be

I cried

the entire
time

it's been three months
since you died
but it felt like yesterday

sometimes
you have to touch the bruise
to heal

**Previously published in The Ravens Perch 10-24-25**

# I Used to Think

I used to think
with you
my scars were invisible

but it just hit me
with you
my scars were infinitely visible

and
you kissed each one, tenderly
till I felt whole, again

**Previously published in The Ravens Perch 10-24-25**

## Nature's Wonder

I love a good
rip-roaring
summer thunderstorm

when the temperature
drops ten degrees
in a matter of minutes

and I'm wrapped up
in a blanket
over my shorts and tee shirt

with an adult beverage to sip
while I watch the sky
and count seconds - between

the earth gets washed clean
in the pouring rain
along with my heart

and the bracing cold
and clink of ice in my glass
warms me, somehow

I breathe deep
of freshness
and wholeness

and the grief
that weighs heavy on my tender heart
takes a back seat

to nature's
nighttime show
of fire and brimstone

the crash of lightning
startling me almost as much as the
boom of thunder

till it waxes and wanes
spent in the beauty
of nature's wonder

**Previously published in The Ravens Perch 10-24-25**

## A Belated Thank You Letter

even
on the darkest days
of my life

there is beauty
to be found there
too

the beauty of the stranger
who was working in the church across the street
from the house where I was living

when it got broken into
when I got broken into
she held my shattered pieces

as I called 9-1-1
and my then-husband
and waited for the ambulance

she didn't worry
that my blood would get on her clothing
and it did

she held me
and prayed for me
and gave me a safe harbor in that tsunami of a day

the day I nearly died, but didn't
18 stitches on a head would
my head wound

inflicted
by two hollowed-out-shells of men
looking for money to buy crack

and the internal wounds
that bled over an entire lifetime
that robbed me of my dignity

she held me
and cradled my heart
and prayed out loud

and there was such beauty
in that stranger
pure, radiant love

that when I think of that day
as I still do now
thirty six years later

I think of that amazing woman
and her unconditional love
and I am profoundly grateful

I wish I had been able
to return to that church later
to thank her

this is my thank you letter
to the beautiful stranger
that terrible day when I nearly died, but didn't

even
on the darkest days
of my life

there is beauty
to be found there
too

**Previously published in GloMag October 2025**

## How Do I Even Begin

how do I even begin
to forgive cancer
for stealing you away

it's been four months
and this is the first time
I've even thought that thought

it would take
a lifetime to accomplish
that forgiveness

**Previously published in GloMag October 2025**

# The Perfect Gift

found the perfect
Christmas gift for you
blue

when I first saw the photo
I clicked on "order"
before it clicked

I'm not
two months early
after all

I will be
forever late ordering
now

**Previously published in GloMag October 2025**

## My Last Thought Every Evening

my last thought every evening
my first thought every morning
you

will there ever come a day
when this is not the case
I doubt it

and
truth be told
I hope not

**Previously published in Lothlorien 12-17-25**

## When I Retire to Michigan

when I retire
to Michigan
when I'm 65

I want to return to
the audacious five year old
who I was

playing with abandon
creating without sensor
loving unabashedly

living in my swimsuit all day
with band aided knees from
bicycle crashes

and believing
in the endlessness
of time and energy

belonging
independent
beloved

my life before me
inside me
all around me

falling asleep
to the cricket song
through my open window

when I retire
to Michigan
when I'm 65

I want to return to
the audacious five year old
who I still am

**Previously published in Lothlorien 12-17-25**

# One Day

one day
at the National Gallery
I stared at
Jean-Baptiste-Camille Corot's painting
so long and
so ardently
that I was inside it

standing at the water's edge
I could feel the breeze
watch the river flowing by
and hear the quiet murmurings
of the few people nearby

time
was suspended
was I there
a moment
or an hour
or a day
I'll never know

but I'll never forget
falling into
Ville-D'avray

that day
at the National Gallery

once fully experienced
a painting
never leaves you

**Previously published in Lothlorien 12-17-25**

# Dinner Tonight

I had dinner tonight
with my new friend,
Adeline

I made a salmon burger
to tempt her out
from her hiding spot
under my bed

and she hopped
onto my lap
and shared a small morsel
of salmon
from my blue plate

and while I read
Mary Oliver
we shared a taste of
togetherness

**Previously published in Lothlorien 12-17-25**

## A Very Full Day

woke after an
odd dream about cats
and names

lovely awakening
writing while the sun rose
to greet me

a poignant church service
with our new pastor
whom I already love

then a zoom call
with poets from
around the world

lovely to
meet them virtually
after four years together

as the call ended
my phone alarm reminded me
of an appointment

driving to the shelter
my heart kept repeating her name
Adeline

I'd fallen in love
with just one picture
overnight

we say on the floor
in your visiting booth
saying hello

when you crawled
in my lapped and purred
I was a goner

bringing you home
was the easiest decision
of a lifetime

as you explored the house
and got settled in
I painted

it is the
largest canvas
I've ever tackled

it's for a friend
and so different
for me

but I loved it
and that lives poured out
and onto the canvas

and when I stood back
and soaked it all in
my heart leapt

and then
I got to spend the evening
connecting with my new friend

when you head butt
me for snuggles
or jump on my lap

the tiny shards of my heart
that were shattered when
my last lives both passed

knit themselves back
together
stronger this time

a few years were shed
in the process of understanding
but fresh love heals

for if grief is love
deep love
with nowhere to go

then aren't I
the lucky one
to have a new love

all this remaining love
with have a vessel in you
and my heart mends itself

what a very full day
of faith and creation
of friendship and new family

of letting go of pain
and risking one's heart
to love again

**Previously published in Lothlorien 12-17-25**

# Even-time

the day floated by
unassuming
diaphanous

I woke to write by candlelight
in the near-dawn gentle light
coffee easing the transition

as light gradually
woke the day, and me
a plan took form

paint
the day awake
eat something to fill the void

return to the shelter
to confirm what my heart already knew
of new love

and then float
on the wings of words
as poetry came into being

connecting with
friends and family
as the day unfolds

I blinked and it went
from AM to PM
with the plan unfurling with ease

Miles Davis on the Bose
welcomes me into even-time
as day turns over to night

**Previously published in Lothlorien 12-17-25**

## Opening My Heart

opening my heart
to the newness of you

reassembling
the pieces of my life
after all the many losses

I have *such love* to give
I have *such deep love*
to receive, to feel

I know you are there
ready, too
to feel my love

my prayer for today
my hope
is that as I'm waking to this new day
and my heart is opening to you
somewhere
you are opening
to me, too

**Previously published in Lothlorien 12-17-25**

# To Brave New Love

opening my heart
to new love
touches the bruise of grief

yet to be able
to feel new love again
I must be brave

it's hard
and tempting to stay
in my shell

but
what's the point
of that

alone
versus the possibility of love
I choose love

**Previously Published in The Ravens Perch 12-21-25**

# Whispering Love

I text you pictures each day, now
of our best times together
to brighten your dark

I gaze into your eyes
in each picture I send
whispering my love

**Previously Published in The Ravens Perch 12-21-25**

# 6-29

typing the date: 6-29
I remember
do you know that I
still have the chopstick wrapper
from that sushi dinner
the day you told me you love me
the first time
ten years ago, now
you know it took you
nearly a year to say it
the first time

I love it that
you used that date
for your email address
I wonder what would happen
if I sent you an email
to that address right now
would anyone get it
or is it already turned off
I'm going to send you an email right now
and send it just because I can
I might even send you this poem

I ordered sushi tonight
from our favorite place
to celebrate
it won't be the same
but it'll be something

**Previously Published in The Ravens Perch 12-21-25**

# Gratitude Spills Out

sitting amidst
the splendor of nature's beauty
my words reform

from heart
to pen to page
they speak

through them
my gratitude for life
spills out

**Previously Published in The Ravens Perch 12-21-25**

# Grief Share

in this circle of love
where everyone around the table understands
I am free to be my authentic self

as my shield comes down
the tears freely flow
an offering of my love

here
my grief mixes with yours
and we heal each other

your wisdom
and perspectives
astound me

each one of you
is so incredibly
brave

and in your eyes
I see my own
braveness, too

such a gift
your insights and
compassion

our hugs are tighter
with the common language
of loss

and the laughter is more real
because we know we must go on
alone, but not truly alone

I leave lighter each week
having laid down the weight of grief
at the foot of your empathy

I cannot imagine
how I would have endured this loss
without you

**Previously published in Ars Nova Shared Visions Anthology 2026**

# Pieces on the Floor

as I
and my heart
lie in pieces on the floor

shattered into
a million tiny shards
after they hear one word:
hospice

the tears freely fall
of their own accord
unbidden
unsummoned
unwanted

and yet
even in the darkness
light begins
to enter into
the spaces between
the broken shards

they are the memories
emerging from the dark
amid the tears

the timeline of just
two or three weeks
is voiced by your lips
and reaches my heart

I thought we'd have
more time
decades, even

one of the bright spots
whispers to me
it's a lucky thing
we lived a lifetime
in only one
decade together

as you slip away
my hardest job
is going to be
learning how
to let you go

I am suspended
between the dark and the light
waiting for the moment
when you are no longer
here

**Previously published in Ars Nova Shared Visions Anthology 2026**

# The Possibility of Joy

looking up
amid the obligations
of the day

I see birds
soaring overhead
clouds
blue sky
beckoning in the distance

I hear bird song
a tender balm
to my parched heart

I feel the warm breeze
and the sun
on my bare skin

I carve space
in my day
to let light in
and I drift up
to the clouds

to soar as one
with the sky

with the birds
with the universe

and in that moment
of lightness and light
I am free
from the bonds of everyday life
from the grief that tethers me

and I float up into
peace
hope
and the possibility of joy

**Previously published in Ars Nova Shared Visions Anthology 2026**

# In the Gloaming

in the gloaming
through the open window
my soul floats freely

in the magic
when day meets night
and fireflies dance

when the warmth of day
wafts over and heats
the coming chill of the evening

when sounds are gentle
muted by the calm
of dusk

it is in this time
of pixie-dust-meets-
imagination

that my heart
connects with all hearts
past, present, future

near and far
real and imagined

and my soul dances
on the thermals
of possibility

**Previously published in Ars Nova Shared Visions Anthology 2026**

# I Breathe

through the glass
of the greenhouse
I sit and feel
the sun's warmth
and I breathe

I breathe out
carbon dioxide
along with
doubt, fear, judgement and grief

I breathe in
oxygen
along with
hope, peace, joy and love

the plants and trees
sustain me

created synergistically
by a loving god
who knows the
beauty of nature
and the frailty of humanity
because he created us
to need each other

as I breathe out despair
and
I breathe in hope

and I say a prayer
of thanksgiving
for each breath

**Previously published in Ars Nova Shared Visions Anthology 2026**

## Tumultuous Waters

of all the bridges
in my life
the one I cherish the most
is you

the tumultuous waters
were raging fast and deep
when we first met

and you created a
path for my steps
to safe shore

over the years
we have had together
time and time again
you were my bridge
my rock
my shore

although I could feel
the rocky waters
churning below me
and feel their foam
splash onto me
knowing I was safe above

on the bridge
that was you
kept me on solid ground

every now and again
I would toss a leaf
over the bridge
watch it fall and flow
downstream
knowing that it
could not
pull me under

now that it is
your time to go
my thoughts drift to wonder
will you be the bridge
that holds me
when the grief
of your passing
threatens to
pull me under?

is it possible
that you
can be the troubled water
and the bridge
to protect me
simultaneously?

there is no one
who can comfort me

from the loss of you
better than you

of all the bridges
in my life
the one I cherish the most
is you

**Previously published in Ars Nova Shared Visions Anthology 2026**

# Mirroring

sky
clouds
trees
lake
dance

sky's reflection
across the lake
trees mirroring each other
in the glassy surface

impossible to know
where one ends
and the other
begins

and as the breeze blows
they twist and turn
in a cloud dance

and I am
in the dance
with them

being twirled
by the trees

standing on the feet of the trees
like I did as a girl
dancing with my dad

the song
of my childhood
begins to play
in the background

I am
a child again
and my heart
is free
dancing with the clouds

**Previously published in Ars Nova Shared Visions Anthology 2026**

## A Tree Beckons

through the doorway
a tree beckons
enter here

come climb
my branches
and explore

come pick my fruit
and be
nourished

come sit
in my shade
and rest

come breathe
and be
filled

leave your worries
behind
inside

and enter here

**Previously published in The Ravens Perch 1-12-26**

# Driving Home

driving home
from your Celebration of Life today
I thought of so many things I could have said

like the time on our first date
when you pulled out the trilogy
of White Dragon Books

that we had talked about before we met
and you said "No matter what happens here,
these are yours."

you had been carrying them
inside your leather jacket
while you rode your Harley to our date

I was blown away
by that gesture
of generosity

it spoke volumes
of your true
character

reader
thinker
giver

and how over the years
we read those very books aloud
to each other

lying end to end
on the couch in your living room
that became our living room

and how you cried
whenever the friendship and love
overwhelmed you

speaking volumes
of the depth of
your heart

the books live
on my dresser
now that you are gone

a bookmark
in the last place
when you read to me

**Previously published in The Ravens Perch 1-12-26**

## Words of Children

the words of children
spoken at memorials
always get me

so earnest and raw
such fresh
innocent grief

**Previously published in The Ravens Perch 1-12-26**

## Empath

my cat
keeps a close eye on me
since you're gone

she notices things
like tears and a
broken heart

they say dogs show empathy
and cats are aloof
which may be true in general

but mine
is the sweetest empath
I've known

purring now
and making biscuits
while I write this poem

these are
her love
languages

**Previously published in The Ravens Perch 1-12-26**

## Now That the Words are Spoken

now that the words are spoken
the prayers prayed
the hugs exchanged

now that the cookies are eaten
the tears dried
the stories shared

now that the chairs are folded
the cars are loaded
and we've gone home

it is slowly seeping in
that you are really
gone

I breathe
and try to open my mind
to let this thought register

it still feels shocking
surreal, unnatural
even now

www.ingramcontent.com/pod-product-compliance
Ingram Content Group UK Ltd.
Pitfield, Milton Keynes, MK11 3LW, UK
UKHW041316190726
13845UKWH00025B/306

9 789363 541481